Repugnicance

The 2012 Version of the Republican ~~Bible~~ Babble

Edited and Curated by

George Won't

Columnist for the *Washington Pissed*

Repugnicance - Version 1.0

Updated: December, 16, 2011

Published by:

The Serendipity Publishing Group

Email: info@serendigity.com

ISBN-13: 978-1468098839

ISBN-10: 1468098837

To join with other Repugnicant Patriots visit:
www.repugnicance.net

Follow Repugnicance on Twitter @Repugnicance

To order additional copies of this book visit:
www.repugnicance.com

For additional information or
for discounts on bulk orders email:
info@repugnicance.com

Table of Contents

Introduction to Repugnicance

REPUGNICANT BABBLE

EXPLAINED IN PLAIN GIBBERISH

REAL QUESTIONS FROM REAL REPUGNICANTS

Stupid Tips for Stupid Repugnicants

In Repugnicant Conclusion

We're Repugnicant ... You occupy the streets. We occupy the corridors of power!

What They're Saying About

Repugnicance

• *Repugnicance* has more bite than a $10 million ad buy. If widely disseminated, it will assure the victory of the Democrats in November 2012.
– Barack Obamma

• *Repugnicance* is the best political parody to come out in years. We will use it as the touchstone of our campaign this Fall.
- David Flouffe

• It's wicked good humor, and chocked full of insight too.
- David Axelrub

• *Repugnicance* is the best book out today on politics. It's got its finger on the pulse of the puffery, the pandering and the political pollution that's filling the airwaves.
- Al Bore

• *Repugnicance* describes in clear and concise babble all BS that Republicans put forth as policy, programs and platitudes.
– Senator John F. Klarity

• Destined to become a classic of political parody.
- The New York Chimes

• If Mark Twain were alive today this is the kind of book he would write.
- USA Tomorrow

• Whoever this George Won't is, he's got the goods on the Repugnicants.
- Dan Blather

• *Repugnicance* captures the ludicrous tone and shriveled spirit of modern day Republicanism.
- Hairy Reed

• Personally I didn't find this book very funny.
- Snit Romney

• Laced with innuendo, factual inaccuracy and hysterical repugnance.
- Snoot Gingrich

• There are three things I didn't like about this book. It was too one sided. It was biased … and … and … I can't remember the third thing. Oops.
- P.Rick Perry

• This book is blasphemy!
- Michele Babblethump

• Just another left leaning hatchet job.
- Hermann Pizza

• Kudos to George Won't for exposing of the gap between the rhetoric and the reality in politics today.
- Good Night Joe

• *Repugnicance* is the McPain straight talk express in book form.
- John McPain

• I've been covering politics for over 30 years and this is the best parody I have ever read … bar none. Spot on!
- Chris Matthoose

• *Repugnicance* is the most insightful book on politics out today. Damn funny too.
- Nancy Peloski

• This book stunk. It's the worst book I ever read. In fact it's the only book I've ever read.

- George B. Wush

• I want to know who this guy George Won't is … so I can congratulate him on a pitch perfect impersonation of perhaps the greatest political commentator of our age.
- George Will

• Todd and I are indignant that this book has been published. It's like a voyeur had camped out on our deck and was peering into our bedroom to get our privately, Repugnicant conversations.
- Saint Sarah

• And you thought Sarah Palin was funny. You've got to read this book.
- Tina Flake

• *Repugnicance* captures what core Republicanism is all about. It shows how money rules in politics … it exposes the game for what it is - a game that's rigged through inside deals financed by lobbyists and campaign contributors. It shows how the 1% to get rich at the expense of the 99%. Then I ask myself, what's wrong with all of that?
- Donald Dump

Introduction by Stephen Coldbeer

When my esteemed colleague at the *Washington Pissed*, George Won't, told me he was working on a top secret project about the Republican candidates, I cringed. "George," I said, "Everything that could possible be put into words about them has already been written."

"That's what I thought to, until I started writing," he said. "Then, I realized that the only real way to understand them is to recreate them. That's recreate as in mental recreation. You simple can't take them seriously, any more."

After reading George's manuscripts, I now know what he meant. These books, like the candidates, are intended as intellectual recreation. George Won't takes the candidates and re-imagines them as:

• Snoot Gingrich,
• Snit Romney,
• Run Paul,
• P.Rick Perry,
• Michele Babblethump,
• Hermann Pizza,
• Saint Sarah and
• Donald Dump.

Repugnicance take the candidates' twisted logic and plays with it … transforming it into a sort of absurd ideology. *Repugnicance* answers over-the-top question from "Real Repugnicants" and provides incisive answers that cut through the BS. *Repugnicance* even provides Stupid Tips for even stupider Repugnicants. All in all, it's a romp.

When I asked George why he had written these Repugnicant books, he told a very revealing story. He said, "When Rick Perry couldn't remember the three departments he proposed to abolish at the Republican debate, I knew we had entered the twilight zone of politics. The next morning, I woke up and a very Repugnicant book was staring me in the face. It started shaking me and shouted, "You're going to write me!"

"No thanks," George said, "I've got more important things to do with my time, slightly exaggerating how valuable his time is.

Repugnicance persisted ... so much so that it e v e n t u a l l y multiplied into two books. According to George, "There may even be further proliferation of *Repugnicance* in my mind."

Repugnicant candidates and their quasi- politico-religion are increasingly dominating the national political debate and it's a philosophy that's nearly impossible to understand. Even worse, you can't avoid it. We can only hope and pray that this isn't a terminal condition for the country.

Eventually George Won't realized that he had no choice in the matter and gave into the creatively destructive urge inside him. He says, "I had to write these books to expose the hypocrisy, the sham and the tragic-comic schizophrenia embodied in what is today put forth by Republicans as political gospel ... a kind of holy babble."

Net Net: George Won't has written two compelling and highly entertaining satires on *Repugnicance*, designed for the Internet age – available both in paperback on Amazon.com and in e-book formats. They're written to try to bring some perspective to what's happened to the Republican Party, and the picture he paints ain't pretty. Fortunately for the nation, the campaign season will soon be over. Unfortunately what happens between now and then … is real.

The first book: *Repugnicants: The Wacky World of Republican Politics.* focuses on the current bumper crop of Repugnicant candidates, their quirks, their personalities and their illogic.

The second book: *Repugnicance: The 2012 Version of The Republican ~~Bible~~ Babble*, focuses on the Repugnicants' world view. It includes a Repugnicant FAQ … a three dot bio of the Repugnicants … and an over-the-top treatment of what passes for a political ideology … carried to the absurd extreme … hopefully getting there before they do.

Now, let me say just a few words about my friend and colleague: George Won't. You might be familiar with the writings of another journalist who, for some time, has been doing a sorry impersonation of George Won't. George Will, the semi-respected columnist for the *The Washington Post*, is absolutely no relation to George Won't. They don't like each other. They don't hag out at the same places. They're light years apart in their political philosophies.

George Won't is the antithesis of George Will. George Will uses proper grammar, correct syntax, impeccable spelling and awesome sentence structure. He even make punctuation an etiquette form. George Won't tends to mangle the English language and hold a deep contempt for spelling. In fact, he considers the punctuation Gestapo the enemy and fires on first sight.

George Will writes for an establishment publication and George Won't is anti-establishment through to the bone. *The Washington Pissed* is not what you might think of as "Inside the Beltway" journalism. Instead you might think of the *Washington Pissed* as the journalistic expression of the citizen anger that has pervaded the larger Occupy movement.

To follow Repugnicance on Twitter (@repugnicance). You can also get fast breaking news about Repugnicance on the Repugnicant Facebook Page and on the blogs that correspond to these two books (www.repugnicance.org and www.repugnicants.org).

Oh and one more thing. Recently I was talking with several students about how Repugnicant things have become in politics today and one of them threw out an idea: "We should have a Repugnicant National Unconvention."

And so an idea was born. Plans are now underway to coordinate a National Repugnicant Unconvention on college campuses the weekend of August 31-Sept 2, 2012, spliced between the Republican and Democratic Conventions. It's conceived as sort of an Occupy Movement for politics … a theatre of the absurd with speeches by the candidates. Will this grow into something grander than the Grand Old Party? Only history can tell. Here's more on the RCU …

THE REPUGNICANT NATIONAL UNCONVENTION

MARK YOUR CALENDAR FOR AUGUST 31 - SEPT 2, 2012

Spliced between the Republican and Democratic Conventions, on the weekend of August 31-Sept 2, 2012, there will be another spectacle called the Repugnicant National Unconvention, taking place on college campuses and select locations around the U.S.A. It will be extremely loosely coordinated by those who **really** don't know what they are doing – the esteemed body aptly dubbed the Repugnicant National Uncommittee. This epochal event will serve as a truly ~~historical~~ hysterical Fall campaign kickoff and an organizing vehicle for something so grand … that … well … even we can't imagine what it might become.

Yes, it's a crazy idea … crazy good. Sometimes crazy is the only appropriate response to a system that has gone crazy on us … as Repugnicance has done. The Repugnicant National Unconvention will be an anti-Republican themed parody culminating in a theatre of the absurd. Students and other slightly touched participants, will play the roles of Republican caricatures like Snoot Gingrich, Mutt Romney, P.Rick Perry, Run Paul and Donald Dump. These caricatures will go through the motions of selecting a nominee for the Repugnicant Party.

There will be music, skewered speeches, bastardized media interviews in one huge and over-the-top parody of Republicans. It's an Occupy Movement for politics ... political theatre for the Internet age. There will be live Webcasts of campus events, local Repugnicant conventions, all around the country. Facebook groups, Twitter news feeds and YouTube postings and major media outreach. Anyone with a wit and a way can participate. Get creative. Use your wits to register your opposition to politics as usual. Our targets? Whoever and whatever the Republicans put forth as a nominee and a platform.

The buildup to the RNU will continue through the Spring and Summer of 2012 using social networks and YouTube videos, photoshopped images, T-shirts, bumperstickers - all the standard and non standard paraphernalia of political campaigning.

On this localized, national stage, the RNU will be programmed for viral growth. The disenchanted and disenfranchised can voice their frustrations in a wry way that detracts major media attention. Our goal is to engage the 99%, who are currently left out of the prevailing political equation.

Just like the GOP convention, the RNU will be strong on bombast and political vacuousness. Speakers will mouth political platitudes like they're Repugnicant gospel. Watch crowds will go berserk over the stupidity of self-serving political ~~prophets~~ profits and repugnant media pundits. Sop up the showmanship as if it were real political spectacle. Delegates will cast their votes for the most vapid candidate and we will have accomplished everything that was accomplished at the real Republican National Convention ... nothing at all.

Although whimsical and wacky, the RNU will also have a serious bite . It will expose the current form of Repugnicance as an absurd abstraction – an over the top political philosophy. We'll skewer the Republican candidates by taking Republican ideas to the extreme outer limits of credibility. All in all we'll create a kind of creative dissonance to the Republican National Convention. Save the date, August 31-Sept 1, 2012 and set the stage for the political theatre in its most rapturous and riotous form. Heck, maybe even George B. Wush and Dick Chicanery will come out from their caves to make guest appearances.

REPUGNICANCE MEANS NOT HAVING TO SAY YOU'RE SORRY ... FOR BEING STUPID.

The Repugnicant National Uncommittee

JOSIAH FRUMPACKER: CHIEF REPUGNICANT: Former Editor in Chief of *The Gaggle* ... hot air balloonist and Squawk Squad Leader. Big voice! Weird sense of humor ... a cutting wit. Especially does't like pretenders!

ANITA MANDALAY - IDEA PERSON: Former waitress at The Blotch in Big Beaver Lick, just down the road from Bible Notch, Texas. A sweetie once you get to know her.

LILY FARNQUIST: POLICY DIRECTOR. Stature belies her quaint demeanor. 5' 2" of sheer might. No holds barred.

HAZLE NUTT - VOLUNTEER COORDINATOR: One Wacky Woman - Moments of civility wrapped in a package of total insanity.

DOTTIE EYES - DIRECTOR OF SYNTAX: Stickler for details. Hired as consultant after the Sarah Palin run-on sentence scandal.

ART CLOGFAART - OUTREACH COORDINATOR: Old Aggie Chum of P.Rick Perry. Part time barber in Paint Creek.

SUZZIE SAUL KNIGHT: OFFICIAL PLANNER Tireless dancer. Formerly with the Blubberhouse Bar in Blunt, South Dakota.

DICK HUNTER - CHIEF RECRUITER: Alway on the lookout for new and exciting talent to beef up the staff.

DR. GASS - OFFICIAL ANESTHESIOLOGIST: Laugh a minute on site physician - Always ready with a gag to take us to new heights.

Balance is the Key to Life

EVAN KEEL - POLICY ANALYST: Thoughtful and well considered position papers that always see two sides to every issue.

HARRY RUMP - OFFICIAL PLUMBER: Expert at fixing leaks in Repugnicance logic. No relation to Joe.

LOIS PRICE - PROCUREMENT SPECIALIST: Bargain hunter supreme. Hired as consultant after Repugnicants got hip to the electorate's fixation with government spending.

FLAY MING ASHOIL - KEEPER OF THE FLAME: International expert … foreign policy supreme … Repugnicance personified.

What is Repugnicance?

• Repugnicance is the Republican ~~Bible~~ babble demystified.

• Repugnicance is the translator between what comes out of the two sides of a Republican's mouth. It exposes of the gap between the rhetoric and the reality of their talking points.

• Repugnicance is extra strength Republicanism.

• Repugnicance is straight talk without any of the blarney that thrown in.

• Repugnicance lays bare the hypocrisy of Republicans, before their consultants dress it up with hot button issues that consultants have gleaned from in depth discussion with Americans in focus groups.

• Repugnicance is what you get when you strip away Republican campaign varnish and the see through to their self serving proposals.

• Repugnicance is what Republicans say to each other in private parties before they open their mouths on the public airwaves.

• Repugnicance is the core Republican philosophy carried to the absurd extreme. It could be the basis of a powerful new movement of anti-Republicanism.

Repugnicants Direct Line to God

Dear God:

Allow us to introduce ourselves. We are Repugnicants and we are the hope of the future, for whatever that is worth to you.

In recent history, Repugnicance hasn't alway been as finely a tuned political religion as it is now. The unfortunate result was the election of Barack Obama, which we all now know was a disaster of epochal proportions.

Of the major political religions, Repugnicance is the only one to emphatically endorses you, as our God as our almighty savior, as so beautifully expressed in the Repugnicant Babble. We are writing you now to ask you to return the favor by endorsing us and show us a sign at the voting booths in November 2012.

SO, NOW WHAT DO WE DO...?

Our positions are like finely chiseled stone sculptures of your only begotten son, Jesus Christ, who died for our political sins on the cross of Democrapic rhetoric. Consider the record:

• We are the only ones to fight for the right for our children to pray in school.
• We are the only ones to recognize that cutting taxes is the Godly thing to do.
• We are the only ones to heed your advice to reduce the size of government.
• We know how sad it makes you feel to see gays serving openly in the military.
• We can see anger in your eyes every time a same sex marriage is performed.
• And did we mention cutting taxes?

We know that you do not always approve of everything that we as humans do. For that reason we ask that you smite Democraps down in their tracks and significantly diminish the amount of traction they gain and especially look askance at their political machine this election cycle. This would be a wise investment of your time and energy. As Repugnicants we are now much more focused, clarity wise, **and** we are also thinking more clearly too about the things that matter most to you.

We, as God fearing Repugnicants, wholeheartedly endorse your position about the importance of faith and fortitude and why learning hard lessons in life is sometimes difficult as articulated so beautifully in the ~~Bible~~ Babble. But we think, ultimately, we are better persons when we have endured the slings and

arrows of misfortune so to speak. For us Repugnicants, we have certainly have done that to the hilt during the trying times of the Obama years.

But now our future is different. Isn't it amazing how far we have progressed since four years ago when Obama was seen as "charismatic" if not a savior.

With a bumper crop of Repugnicant candidates, we are now at the top of our game, demonstrating unusual political savvy in our dealings with the gotcha media and political sickos, not to mention the voters themselves who we are now inculcating the voting electorate with our ideas, religious dogma and political philosophy. Towards that end, we are herewith releasing a pre-publication draft of our movement's biographical book, and we would like to invite you to write an introduction to this masterpiece. The sales of this book will surely will be millions so it's a good way for you to get your message out to the masses. If you will do this for us, we will all be very proud of you.

In the meantime, we are plunging ahead with various additional ideas and tax cuts plans, including one put forth by the inestimable Snoot Gingrich, in which households making more than $1 million a year would see their taxes drop by an average of 62 percent, which will be a huge boost to your Supply Side Economics religion.

We're not only strong on the economy. We have ideas in foreign policy, health care, socialism. We would also like to hear from you. We are also prepared to invite you to make a major foreign policy address at the Repubnicant National Unconvention, August 30-September 2, 2012. We will pay your round trip airfare to and from heaven, plus a six figure speaking fee. This is not some pie in the sky proposal.

Our passionate supporters will pack a football stadiums and basketball arenas

around the country to hear your thoughts. Some of our political supporters say they know you and speak very highly of your exploits throughout history. Others, who we call our "associates," are active in the political campaign arena, and religious circles that you approve of. We believe that our movement has what it takes to succeed, politically and economically and spiritually. Being spiritually savvy people, we know that your support for us could be instrumental in our victory at the ballot box in November 2012.

What do you say? Will you join our team?

Sincerely yours,

The Repugnicants

PS: Do you want and write the introduction to our book?

GOD'S AUTHENTIC REPLY!

Dear Friends in the Repugnicant Movement:

At this critical juncture in evolution of humanity, I am concerned. I can clearly see that we need something dramatic to shift the course of history. I am prepared to take extreme remedial action to that effect. That's why I look kindly upon the creation of a new and improved Repugnicance brand political philosophy. I knew that if humanity was to survive, a new kind of wisdom and a much more potent quasi religious - political movement must be thrust on the world stage.

Accordingly I have decided, for the first time in the history of the world, to endorse a political party in the upcoming election for President. I believe it is incumbent on me as God let the masses know where I stand and unequivoate by endorsing your movement, which you have so aptly name, Repugnicance. I fervently believe that Repugnicance can and will be the **Salvation of humanity**.

BUT .... LET ME EMPHASIZE ... ALL IS NOT PEACHES AND CREME IN POLITICS THESE DAYS. Take for example ObamaCare.

Thus, even with my endorsement, your assured victory is not a slam dunk. ... even with Obama's approval ratings in the shitter. Between you and me, I also have a Plan B. If the election in 2012 does not work out as we hope, I am prepared to take extreme karmic action in retribution. Watch out!

It is with these cosmic concerns in mind that I step forth in my support for Repugnicance. In other words, I have decided to endorse the Repugnicance Party's candidate for President in 2012, be it Snoot Gingrich, Snit Romney, or even fringe candidates like P.Rick Perry, Michele Babblethump, Run Paul or (God forbid) Donald Dump. You may use this letter as evidence to this effect. I have attached a copy of my introduction which you may attribute to me in your forthcoming book …. which I understand is the new Holy ~~Bible~~ Babble.

Sincerely yours,

God

Introduction by God

I AM WARNING YOU HUMANS ... 2012 IS NOT GOING TO BE BUSINESS AS USUAL. IGNORE MY WORDS AT YOUR PERIL. WAKE UP TO REPUGNICANCE BEFORE IT'S TOO LATE.

In other words, the world is rapidly approaching "reckoning of sorts," AKA "The Time of Trial on Earth,

Perhaps you have already reached the reckoning. The data is unclear.

A "reckoning" is the moment at which people start to freak out and logic starts to decline precipitously until all that is left is Democrapic Blarney. Is there an alternative to this dire scenario? Yes!

Believe in Repugnicance! Believe the real facts about unreality. Listen to the Profits I have sent to spread my words to the masses. Believe in the Gospel according to Snoot Gingrich. Believe in the Gospel according to Snit Romney. Believe in the Gospel according to P.Rick Perry. Believe in the Gospel according to Bombshell Bachmann. Believe in the Gospel according to The Donald. Believe in these Profits and you will believe anything.

This is the Repugnicant Babble. This book is the authentic interpretation of my words according to the Supply Side Prophesy ... the factual basis of true Repugnicance.

Ignore Repugnicance at your peril. If you fail to heed the words of the Repugnicant Profits, a catastrophe of historic proportions awaits you humanoids. Historians, the ones who were smart enough to board the ark, will one day look back and ask, "Why didn't God say something about this? Why didn't he do something before it was too late?"

The Ten Commandments of Repugnicance

THE ALMIGHTY DOLLAR IS THE LORD YOUR GOD AND HATH BROUGHT YOU OUT OF THE HOUSE OF BONDAGE.

$ ONE: Thou shalt have no other gods besides the Almighty dollar.

$ TWO: Thou shalt make for thyself a campaign image --t he likeness of which is everything on television, or that is on the Internet, or that is in the media in any form.

$ THREE: Thou shalt not take the name of Supply Side Economics in vain.

$ FOUR: Thou shalt remember the election day, and keep it holy.

$ FIVE: Thou shalt honor thy lobbyists and thy campaign contributors.

$ SIX: Thou shalt murder any legislation proposed by Democraps.

$ SEVEN: Thou shalt commit ideological adultery.

$ EIGHT: Thou shalt steal from government coffers.

$ NINE: Thou shalt bear false witness against Democraps.

$ TEN: Thou shalt covet thy lobbyists campaign contributions; Thou shall covet thy lobbyists wallet, his portfolio, his car, his corporate jet, his vacations, and anything that is thy lobbyists.

The Repugnicant 2012 Yearbook

Three ... Dot ... Bios ... of the
Repugnicant ... Candidates

Snit Romney - The Panderer

The candidate without a character ... the politician without a personality ... formerly the bane of Venture Capital ... bought early into in Staples: The Office Superstore, but now wants to stupefy the entire Oval office ... says he understands how the economy works ... but has only seen how it works from the top down ... specialized in buying companies and firing their employees ... now says he's an expert in creating jobs ... Mormon missionary work in France helped shape his character ... now trying to fit the rounded shape of Mormonism into the square holes of fundamentalist Christians ... saved the Olympics from disgrace by selling it to socially irresponsible sponsors like Nike ... flip flopper supreme ... switches positions every hour on the hour ... now disavows any connection to the ObamaCare health care system he instituted en Mass ... father was CEO of American Motors ... son wants to be CEO of American Inc ... attended exclusive Cranberry School in Bloomfield Hills where every student is plum ... father was Governor of Michigan ... he would have done the same but took the wrong turn out of Haarvid Yard ... owns so many blind trusts he can no longer see straight ... but the super story on Snit is the time

he drove his wife and kids on a 12-hour journey to Canada with their freaked-out Irish setter strapped to the roof of the family station wagon in a box the story catapults Snit to the top echelons of American politics. Does it get any better than this?

Snoot Gingrich - The Professor

Politician without principles … the nutty professor whose ideas are even nuttier … wants inner city kids to clean of the crap of their classmates so they can develop a fondness for work … big proponent of space exploration so more space cadets like him can find work … says he divorced his first wife because she wasn't pretty enough to be the wife of a good looking President … like who … Snoot? … yeah right! … told the Occupy Wall Street protesters to take a bath before getting a job … they told him to go jump in a lake … serial adulterer … kicked off his candidacy for the irony Hall of  Fame by signing the Defense of Marriage Pledge … what? …. has had almost as many wives as ethics violations … with a totally straight face says he has never changed his positions in Congress as a result of taking money from corporate interests … yeah, like they were just giving to charity … expected nothing in return … proffered advice to Fannie Mae for a cool $30,000 per month … $1.6 million for telling them what not to do … engineered the takeover of the House with his Contract With America … now seeks takeover of the White House with his contract on America … fashions himself as an expert historian … cites his similarities to Ronald Reagan as evidence of this knowledge … what's wrong with this picture? According to knowledgeable sources, they couldn't find a football helmet in his high school large enough to fit his big fat head…. while he was having an extramarital affair he railed against Bill Clinton for doing the same thing … claims President Obama is "so outside out comprehension that you can only understand him in the context of the anti-colonial behavior imparted by his father … despite the fact that Obama has never lived in Kenya and met his father only once … had to pay $300,000 in penalty for his ethics violations while Speaker of the House … but considers it a good investment for what he got in return … feels a passionate love for this country and in particular the women in it with whom he had affairs … refers to himself as a transformational figure … but meant to say he's a transfigured formation.

P.Rick Perry - The Clown

Stole the show in the Repugnicant debates with his clown act ... couldn't remember what he couldn't remember ... master at flubbing his lines ... former Aggie Squawk Squad leader ... majored in animalism ... rumored to

be Gay ... but squelched the rumors by coming out strong against Gay rights ... a real man of unreal principles ... so principled he double dips his salary taking retirement pay while still working to cut salaries of his staff ... admirer of Fed Chairman Bernanke ... extended an open invitation for him to attend a Texas barbecue and be the guest roast ... a devout Christian who holds masses for tens of thousands in Texas football stadiums, but denies any political intentions ... even though he's running for President ... says he created millions of jobs for Texas ... but the state ranks near the bottom in education ... and everything else that it takes to create skilled workers ... came out of the gate strong in the nomination process ... lead in polls for a few weeks ... then the Repugnicant piranhas started eating his flesh ... attacked his immigration stance ... debate performances didn't help ... reacted by going on late night comedy talk shows ... his camp became camp ... speech in New Hampshire became an instant YouTube hit ... looked like he was either drunk or stupid ... you choose ... outdid himself with his Broke Mountain TV ad attacking gays in military ... another YouTube sensation ... the man has a way with viral distribution ... but not words ... destined to become the greatest road show since Saint Sarah ... great sense of humor ... most likely to succeed at stand up comedy ... could have a great career ahead of him ... outside politics.

MicheleBabbleThump - The Looney

Ms Crazy Eyes ... stole the spotlight from Saint Sarah ... once the Tea Party darling ... hates Crony Capitalism ... adopted 23 children ... all teenage girls ... imagine their slumber

parties ... she and her husband

provide short term care for girls with eating disorders ... by serving them cake ... her home is legally classified as a "treatment home" ... so she doesn't have to go outside to get treated anymore ... very useful in those cold Minnesota winters ... loves the book, *Total Truth: Liberating Christianity from Its Cultural Captivity*" ... wants to liberate the rest of America from it's cultural captivity ... she and her husband are professional Christian counselors ... charging customers to tell them what to believe ... great work if you can get it ... unfortunately neither Michele nor her husband are licensed psychologists in Minnesota ... whatever ... denies ever having done "conversion therapy" which attempts to transform gays into "normal people" ... but hidden camera exposed that they really do it at their clinics ... her income statements reveal that she accepted earning of upwards of $100,000 from a farm owned by her father in law ... that received between $260,000 in federal crop subsidies between 1995 and 2008 ... public pro-life protester ... not afraid of a good fight ... challenged Snoot in debates ... Snoot challenged her facts ... she challenged Snoot's veracity ... Snoot challenged her stability ... great theatre ... it can only get better from here ...

Run Paul - The Radical

Radical ideas that appeal to rabid supporters ... stable support from unstable supporters ... can raise money without the Repugnicant Party ... but can't break out of single digits ... why? ... wants to abolish the Fed and replace it with ... what? ... well, he'll figure that out later ... says U. S. can't be the policeman of the world any more ... good point ... same good point he's been making for 30 years to deaf ears ... perhaps it's the messenger ... libertarian leanings ... just how far he leans ... nobody's sure ... but definitely near the tipping point ... termed "The Godfather of the Tea Party Movement" but not sure whether that's a compliment ... trained as a physician ... but in the 60's he was influenced by Friedrich Hayek's *The Road to Serfdom*, Ludwig von Mises and Ayn Rand.

... came to know the Austrian school economists well ... so well that August 15, 1971, when President Richard Nixon "closed the gold window" Paul decided to enter Texas politics, ... the clincher was that now "all money would be political money rather than money of real value." today this underscores all his views ... served 12 terms in Congress ... but still believes in term limits ... continues to blame the Fed for hidden taxes through inflation ... and wants Congressional pay cuts ... in 1984, he decided to retire to run for the U.S. Senate, but lost the primary ... his House farewell address pulled no punches, "Special interests have replaced the concern that the Founders had for general welfare. Vote trading is seen as good politics. ... in the 1988 presidential election, Paul was on the ballot in 46 States as the Libertarian Party candidate ... did okay got 432,179 votes representing less that 1% of the total vote ... today he actually leads in some polls from time to time ... a real loner amongst Repugnicants ... actually reads books.

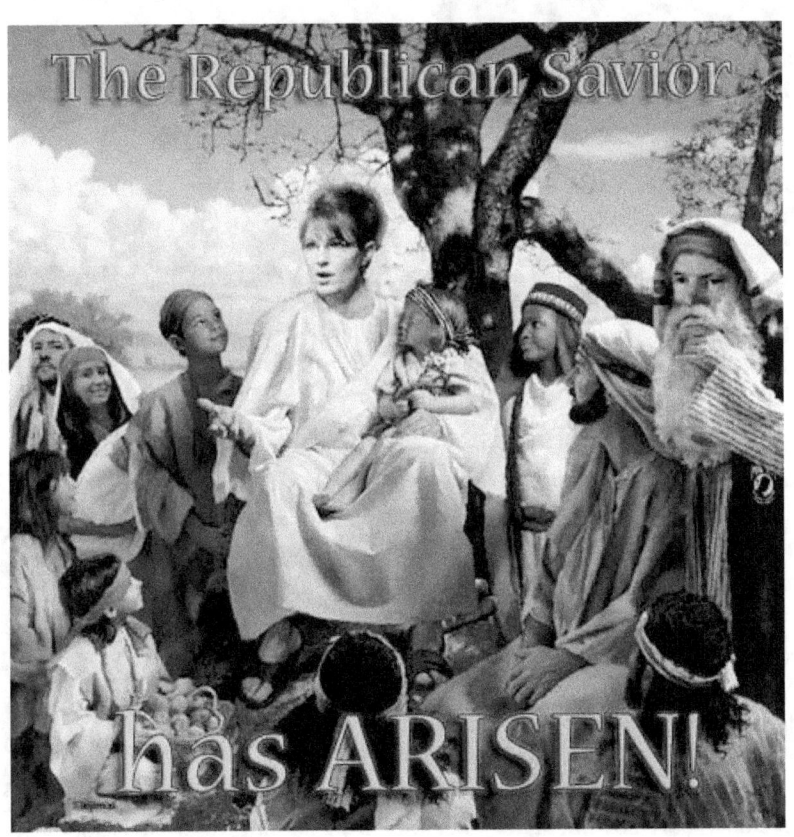

A Brief History of Repugnicance
As seen from the Heavens

It all started one day when I was flying my hot air balloon above the terrain of Texas. Floating almost a mile above from the earth, I looked below and saw what

appeared to be a message from God. *"It was a sign."* I said to myself. *"Sarah Palin's likeness had been implanted unto the earth."* I'm not one to quibble with direct messages from God. I said to myself, "I have seen the light but what is the message?"

Pronto, I got God on the wire and asked, "What exactly are you telling us?"

God said, "I'm telling you that Sarah Palin is the Godmother of a new Movement - The Repugnicance Movement.

Slow going doesn't even begin to describe how things developed in the nascent stages of this burgeoning movement. "At first I was the only one who thought Repugnicance had a prayer to become a major movement. It was not easy, recruiting all the consultants, big time media support and institutional funding. But the turning point came when I met Anita Mandelay at the Big Beaver Lick Baptist Church. We immediately connected over Repugnicance fusion of politics and religion. Then and there I decided to make Anita the official Repugnicance movement recruiter. That was the turning point in our turnaround. Suddenly our humble organization started getting bigger and bigger. It was a miracle. Will historians one day look back analyze the reasons for Repugnicance's meteoric rise in the galaxy of politicaldom? If so, I

believe all the credit goes to Anita Mandalay. She inspired all of us. She was catalyst for expanding our movement membership from nothing to what is today ... even more than nothing. We believe that all this is the foreplay of God's will acting through the embodiment of Repugnicance in human history.

Saint Sarah

The Mother of All Repugnicants

Sarah Louise Heath Palin was invited to join the tribe of humanity on a snowy laden mid Winters day in February 11, 1964 and in short order became an outstanding leader and statesperson in the tradition of other

American heroes and heroines like Abraham Lincoln, George Washington and Ronald Reagan, not all of whom rose as astronomically as Sarah, serving as Governor of Alaska from 2006 until she opted in her resignation in 2009 to the great state of Alaska as Governor being elected in 2006, rising up through the ranks of politicaldom as an upstanding member of the Weasel, Alaska, city council starting from 1992

and continuing up into and through 1996 including   being the mayor from 1996 to 2002, and unfortunately losing her unsuccessful bid for Lieutenant Governor of Alaska in 2002, however not discouraged and deflated by this unsightly turn of events, she still had the gumption to plough ahead with her life (for this is the stuff of what heroines are made) and soon she chairwomaned the Alaska Oil and Gas Conservation Commission from 2003, but decided to resignate in 2004, which of course opened up the door to her election as Governor, by the way the states first female governor not to mention youth ... as   the youngest person ever elected governor of the Alaskan State of the Union. Was this God's will? We have our beliefs about this of course. We believe that God fully participates in a spiritual manner of speaking in the lives of all conservatives, which Sarah Palin exemplifies to the hilt, including her membership in church activities of her choosing, but really being Godlke in her being and acting on God's wishes through her, her actions, words, deeds and other things that she perpetrated through her increasing stardom on the national stage of politics, literary famousness, and her book, which we believe is a masterpiece, without even having read a word of it so far, and most people don't read books these days, preferring mobile devices with wireless Internet browsers not to mention the Kindle and the new Nook of Barnes and Noble, which by the way will include versions of our book as well as Sarah Palin at a reasonably priced discount for conservatives who support us in our literary endeavors, but back to Sarah Palin and her bio, which is amazing if you think about it from basketball Barracuda to VEEP and maybe Presidential candidates to boot depending on the polls and election results. The question becomes just how soon is it until Sarah Palin engraves herself in the mountain of historical memorabilia with other greats in Presidential Politics.

Sarah Palin has clearly been thrust upon the national Mountaintop with other Political Giants.

Saint Sarah - Early Years

Sarah Palin first entered the world through the holy entrance of her mother's womb in Sandpoint, Idaho, having been beaten to the punch by two older siblings who had the honor of being born first to Sarah and Charles R. Heath, who by the way was a respected science teacher and track coach, while his wife did secretarial work for school.   It wasn't long until the Heath family uprooted themselves altogether and opted for the somewhat rural back roots town of Weasel and did we mention that Weasel High School, where Sarah attended is an integral part of the Matanuska-Susitna Borough School District know best for it head football coach Jim Shitter who was honored with selection to the National Football League's Youth Summit in Canton, Ohio. Shortly thereafter around the 2007 timeframe, Shitter lead the school's football team to their first playoff appearance in five seasons just a few years after, teacher Anthony R. Jensen became a James Madison fellow for being a distinguished history teacher, Meanwhile back to Sarah Heath, who was the ringleader of the Fellowship of Christian Athletes, and a spry member of the girls' cross country team, but the big thing was being captain and scrappy

point guard of the school's girls' basketball team which smothered other teams with tight defense - barracuda Heath stealing balls all over the court while winning the Alaska state championship in 1982, fair and square against other teams with players who were bigger than "Barracuda" but it was her competitive streak that distinguisher her from other basketball players without such a completive streak.

The Education of a Saint

Sarah graduated herself by her bootstraps in 1982 from Weasel High School, and quickly made a reputation for herself about town at the Miss Weasel

pageant, possibly moving up to become Miss Alaska and Miss America, but let's not get ahead of ourselves because she only finished third in the 1984 Miss Alaska pageant, but we add parenthetically, receiving the distinguished honor "Miss Congeniality" (I loved that movie with Whatshername) .... But still Sarah got a college scholarship to Hawaii Pacific University in the Fall of 1982, not satisfied with lollygagging on the beach, Sarah instead transferred herself to North Idaho College winning the distinguished Alumni of the Year award, but not until later when she became famous in June of 2008 ... but it was the move in the Spring and Fall of 1983 to the University of Idaho and then onto , Matanuska-Susitna College in the Fall of 1985, and the University of Idaho again in the Spring and Fall of 1986 and the Fall of 1987, when she triumphantly received her Bachelor's degree in communications with an emphasis in journalism having exhausted all the possible colleges and maybe setting a record for college trotting, we're not sure about that.

Nascent Beginnings of a Political Dynamo

Sarah Palin's political beginnings began over her burgeoning views about public finance and of revenues that were flowing like waves in a sea crashing upon a new Weasel sales tax. Was this wise? Sarah became convicted over her strong feelings about this. As a consequence she won handily benefiting from 530 votes to 310 in her election to the city council of Weasel Alaska in 1992. With this as an auspicious beginning, she ran once again for reelection in 1995, winning this time even more impressively, amassing 413 votes to 185 for the opposition. She was on an upward trajectory political wise now and did not complete her second term on the city council in favor of her election to mayor of Weasel in 1996. Sagaciously, she registered with the Repugnicants and ran officially in this political affiliation of her party thenseforth.

As Mayor of Weasel, she served two three-year terms for a total tenure of six years (1996–2002) most of this time as the mayor of the same town. (Weasel) In 1996, she defeated three-term incumbent mayor John Stein, platforming on the issues of waste in spending and high taxes, not to mention her strong opposition to women having chosen abortion over other alternative means of abstinence including gun rights, and term limits and other campaign matters. By now Weasel was growing by leaps and bounds with a total census clocked in at 6,300 residents only a few of which really cared about things like politics. The tax cuts were a big deal however, because many big box stores created the infrastructural improvements necessary to stimulate Weasel's booming economy with an estimated 50,000 shoppers a day. Clearly she was a star on the rise now with national media attention just a few heartbeats away in the scope of national and international affairs.

Political Battles She Singlehandedly Fought and Won With Her Bare Hands

During her first year in office, Palin kept a jar with the names of Weasel residents on her desk. Once a week, she plucked a name from it and dialed them on the telephone asking: "How's the Weasel doing?" And she was savvy with finances too. Using hard earned income generated by a 2% sales tax that was enacted before she was elected to the city council, Palin cut property taxes by 75% and eliminated personal property and business inventory taxes. Using municipal bonds, she single handedly improved roads and sewers, and bolstered law and order in Weasel through Police Departments and other means. She also personally built new bike paths and storm-water treatment facilities, while raising a family and smiling like it was nothing at all.   At the same time, the city reduced spending on the town museum and stopped construction of a new library and city hall because of the tax and spend ways of predessors in the town of Weasel power structure old boy network.

During her second term as mayor, Palin introduced a ballot measure proposing the construction of a municipal sports center to be financed by a 0.5% sales tax increase.[50] The $14.7 million Weasel Multi-Use Sports Complex was built on time and under budget, but the city spent an additional $1.3 million because of an eminent domain lawsuit caused by the failure to obtain clear title to the property before beginning construction. The city's long-term debt grew from about $1 million to $25 million through voter-approved indebtedness of $15 million for the sports complex, $5.5 million for street projects, and $3 million for water improvement projects. A city council member defended the spending increases as being caused by the city's growth during that time.

Stepping on the National Stage

By now everyone and cat knows that in 2008, Repugnicant presidential candidate, John McPain took what has been called a risky bet and placed it on the nose of Sarah Palin as his running mate in that year's

presidential election, making her only the second female candidate for national presidential or vice presidential parties as well as Alaskan first to fill the national ticket, as well as the first female vice-presidential nominee of the Repugnicant Party but unfortunately for all involved the stinging defeat of the McCain-Palin ticket ended in sour fashion especially all the back and forth about she did this ... or tit for tat ... basically trying to detract from her excellent potential as a longer term candidate for President in the Repugnicant presidential nomination in 2012, which totally spun out of control media wise when on July 3, 2009, Palin went public with the announcement that she would not seek reelection to be governor again instead choosing to write her book so she had to resign, which effectively was a good business decision because it would have be time consuming (and then some) to run Alaska while writing a biographical book about herself, despite having just eighteen months prior starting her first term and not to mention the numerous ethics complaints and resultant legal bills affected her ability to govern the state without going into debt so you can see she has had her plate full for awhile. But back to the issues at hand. Sarah Palin's detractors argue that she was only the VEEP candidate on a handicapped ticket of MaCain with the top slot, and therefore could not overcome the deficiencies that he brought to the ticket.   Does this argument hold water? What about holy water?   Nuff said.

REAL QUESTIONS
FROM
REAL REPUGNICANTS

REPUGNICANT
BABBLE EXPLAINED
IN PLAIN GIBBERISH

WHAT ARE SOME REPUGNICANT POSITIONS ON FOREIGN POLICY?

• Question From: Andrew Babcock, Housepainter, Sioux City, Iowa

THE TRUTH ACCORDING TO THE REPUGNICANT BABBLE:
Repugnicants believe that we are rapidly approaching "peak chaos in the world." Perhaps we have already reached it. The data is unclear. Peak chaos signals the moment at which the maximum supply of chaos is reached and global confusion starts to increase exponentially. Common sense starts to decline in reverse proportionality. Peak chaos also signals that God emphatically states to humankind,

"Hold it folks, I will no longer support you in the way I have done in the past." Will these factors affect America's status as a world leader and our ability to sustain economic growth on a par with the growth in deficits? If not, a world crisis and an economic reckoning of epic proportions awaits us. Will historians one day look back at this moment in time and say, "You blew it folks! Repugnicance believes there is a better way to organize world affairs based upon the Repugnicance Pax Americana. Details will be forthcoming as the 2012 election proceeds precariously forward."

What Are the Key Planks in the Repugnicant Platform?

• Question By: Martha Kempis, Grocery Store Clerk, Flat Creek, Kentucky

The Truth According to The Repugnicant Babble: Think 5 Gs!

God: Repugnicance, God fearing Repugnicants, support God wholeheartedly in his various endeavors and policy initiatives despite what atheists and non believers believe.

Guns: Repugnicant gunslingers support the rights of all red blooded Americans to carry and shoot as many guns as they want at whatever they want so including shooting holes through The Constitution.

Gays: Repugnicance holds that a man and a woman are just that and not to be confused with other kinky behaviors in bed or whatever.

Gold: When will our government raise itself from the specter of fiscal irresponsibility with the looming demise of the dollar so best to place your hard earned deposits in gold.

Government: Enough is enough and too much is too much. When government becomes part of the problem that it's trying to solve, then you have a rubrics' cube of dissonance that, in the end, serves no one but the pork barrels and their lobbying cronies inside the beltway.

WHY IS MODERN POLITICS
SO REPUGNICANT?

• Question From: Gertrude Wister, Air Traffic Controller, San Jose, CA

THE TRUTH ACCORDING TO THE REPUGNICANT BABBLE:

It's a fact of modern political life that when a powerful force like Repugnicance arrives on the scene, everybody wants to become part of movement. This would be fine, except different people have different ideas about what Repugnicance means inaction. There are those who feel action means inaction. Some think it's the reverse. For others it means taking the "bull of change" by the horns. Down here inside Repugnicance Power Bunker, we believe that it can't be both without getting splinters. Other folks at other fractured groups within the grander Repugnicance movement (namely: The Tea Party ... essentially a marginal, splinter faction) don't believe anything that can't be proved. Some Repugnicants are even flip floppers believing against all dictates of common sense, that they can have it both ways and still get theirs.

GOP field comes into focus

This is just nonsense! Stick-to-it-ness is what strong leadership is all about. We call upon Repugnicants to stand up and say to our minions, "Enough!" We need to take Democraps out behind the woodshed, metaphorically speaking and give them a stern talking to about not increasing socialist tendencies, not to mention miscreants like unnamed individuals who last name begins with Obama or Clinton. By the way this statement contains no implications about possible kinky behavior, but the sordid and sultry facts (and related details, which I'm not at liberty to enumerate upon) speak for themselves. This is just not proper and if word gets out about it in the larger sphere of media centricism, then it could have a backlashing effect on the prominence of our movement. ... Nuff said!

HOW DO REPUGNICANTS FEEL ABOUT HEALTH CARE REFORM?

• Question From: Eleanor Throttlemeyer, Second Grade Teacher, Bloomington, IN

THE TRUTH ACCORDING TO THE REPUGNICANT BABBLE:

The health care debate centers on one overriding issue that trumps anything else: do we want good health care or not? Is so then why do we let Democraps, industry insiders and lobbyists for insurance companies ram down our throats an a misguided and convoluted 3000 pages of gibberish to pass a sweeping government takeover of health care since we are committed to fix what is broken, especially when tax hikes are involved in creating "Death Panels" that will decide the fate of your life with a government takeover of health care, paid for with more than $800 trillion or more in new tax hikes and that will destroy 5.5 billion jobs.

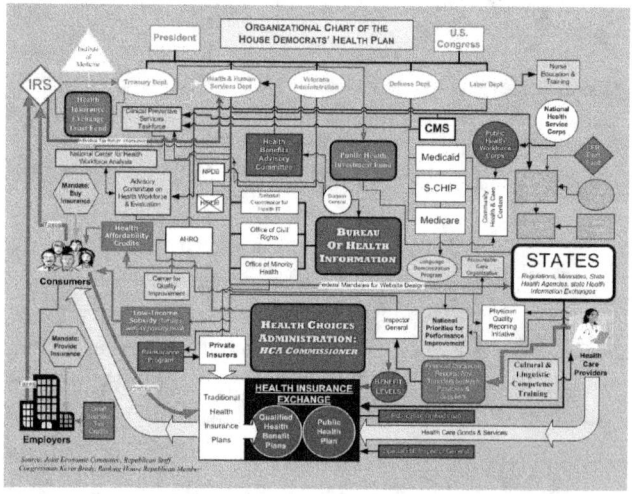

That's what we're up against in this debate. An independent analysis by the Grope Group found that as many as 184 billion Americans would lose their current health insurance. The president and Democraps in Congress need to start over on their health care plan. Reasonable Repugnicants are ready to work on bipartisan solutions to health care reform, but ...

Enough is enough!!!!!!!!!!!!!!!!

Why is Everyone Now Talking about Repugnicance?

• Question From: Brigham Young Jr., Preowned Car Salesman, Fillmore, Utah

The Truth According to The Repugnicant Babble:

It is natural that a movement as powerful as Repugnicance would magnetize a certain amount of both attraction and criticism, especially from those marginalized and radical leftist groups who might not have such amazing potential in the political sphere and possible talk show hosting. But what we have seen in the way of Democrapic gangbustering is simply beyond the beyond. What do they hope to prove by saying that Repugnicance is not what everyone thinks he is? Even more to the point, do they seek to prove that Repugnicance is what everyone thinks it is? Either way, what are they proving? We call upon all red blooded Americans to stand up and stop this nonsense before Democrapic rhetoric blots out all semblance of progress in the great country. Call them out … now!

Can I be Saved By being Repugnicant?

• Question From: Isabel Saggucci, Flowergirl, Faro, TX

THE TRUTH ACCORDING TO THE REPUGNICANT BABBLE:
Emphatically yes! God has made his endorsement clear. (See "Authentic" letter from God in the beginning of this babble) as irrefutable evidence to this effect. But this still begs the question, what can you do to please God even more in the way of

support for Repugnicance. As the picture above illustrates, the path of getting saved requires that you are willing to walk across the narrow bridge above a fog of doubt and despair. This is the point we find ourselves in, as we make the hard political choices that face our great nation. Some people doubt Repugnicance's staying power on the stage of history. You must cast aside this doubt and walk across this bridge to a better nowhere that awaits us in Repugnicance land. Remember that all the great leaders of the world were once unknowns with little foreign policy experience and even less executive know how. Repugnicance is a sure fire political ideology. We know what it takes to be saved in a world of atheists, non functional disbelievers and doubters who will not be saved unless the get with the program and support Repugnicance, whatever level of sense may be embodied in our fervent beliefs.

How soon will the World End?

• Question From: Gail Baker, Dog Walker, Sante Fe, New Mexico.

The Truth According to The Repugnicant Babble:

It depends! There are positive signs that may forestall the end of the world for at least a few more years, 10 years tops. If we are not careful, this timetable could be speeded up. President Obooma is not helping things. This fact was substantiated by Pastor Sedgewick Snodgrass in his sermon delivered to the Coon Creek Baptist Church, on the occasion of God's attendance in the front row pew much to the rapture of the other churchgoers. In a nutshell, what Pastor Snodgrass said was that we can't take the continuance of the future for granted. He explained that eternity, in a technical sense is just beginning. But on a deeper analysis, God is not specific about eternities entry point and exit point in time. If it happens that we are about to exit from eternity prematurely than what is there to prevent that from happening

without **any** advance notice? See the picture to the left to realize just how close we are now to this possible exit point from eternity. The implications of this are profound. We must recognize that our decisions now will affect what happens henceforth. We have the power to control the future because God's will is based upon our choice of the paths that lie before us. We can either choose to be pessimistic about the future or choose the more optimistic brand of Repugnicance. The choice is up to you.

What does it mean to Become a Repugnicant Patriot and How Can I Become One?

• Question From: Ellen Reisters, Waitress, Tampa, Fl

The Truth According to The Repugnicant Babble: Many Americans wonder what they can do to become better at not knowing anything.

A Repugnicant Patriot is someone who completely and uncritically subscribes to the premium grade stupidity inherent in the Repugnicance Paradigm.

To learn more about how you become a Repugnicant Patriot and in the process get discounted quantities of Premium Grade American stupidity, visit our Website at www.Repugnicance.com and join our RP Brigade, and start carrying our specially designed MRM weapon. (Metaphorical Repugnicant Machete)

Is Repugnicance Godlike?

• Question From: Joe Patterson, Sheet Metal Worker, Detroit, MI

The Truth According to The Repugnicant Babble:

Not only is Repugnicance Godlike … Repugnicance is God, incarnated? Why else did God create Repugnicance as his only given political philosophy? God often hires ghosts, saints and decibels to do the heavy lifting on earth so that he can concentrate on improving heaven. So too it is with Repugnicance and our ghosts. This Repugnicance ~~Bible~~ Babble contains of some of the imponderables that we urge you to consider in considering who to trust. Either way we believe that blasphemy is nothing to be sneezed at.

In the Repugnicance Movement we believe that our saints have not only been anointed by God and history to lead us to the promised land of Repugnant Bliss. But we believe that Repugnicance is also God's will incarnate. There is a close bondage here. God is God. Repugnicance is Repugnicance …. They are one and the same. Remember Repugnicance is God … and because of this we cannot lose the election? Besides everybody knows that God is a a Repugnicant. Just ask God. He knows!

Do You have any Special training Programs for Repugnicance?

• Question From: Roger McDonald, Radio Personality, Seattle, WA

THE TRUTH ACCORDING TO THE REPUGNICANT BABBLE: Currently the "Staff" of The Repugnicance Movement is organizing and training "swat squads" of Repugnicant stupids designed to spread the gospel of Repugnicance. You can learn more and study the tutorials on how to embrace our mission by visiting our Spiffy new Website at www.repugnicance.com. We also organize classes in "Stupidity Bonding" including fun filled role playing experiences, that emphasize increasingly essentiality, regarding the true potentiality of Repugnicance in the larger sphere of Repugnicant-World Bi-Focal Americana, taught by some of the greatest Repugnican luminaries of the 21st century.... Including the hero of all stupid Americans below.

STUPIDITY...

Doesn't stop some people.

Does The Repugnicance Movement have a Tutorial?

• Question From: Daniel Magolis, Bar Bouncer, St. Louis, MO

The Truth According to The Repugnicant Babble:
Our tutorial is very simple. It begins with one question,

"May we help you to be more stupid?"

To advance our tutorial motto we have developed an exercise to help you advance. To start taking our tutorial please follow the instructions below...

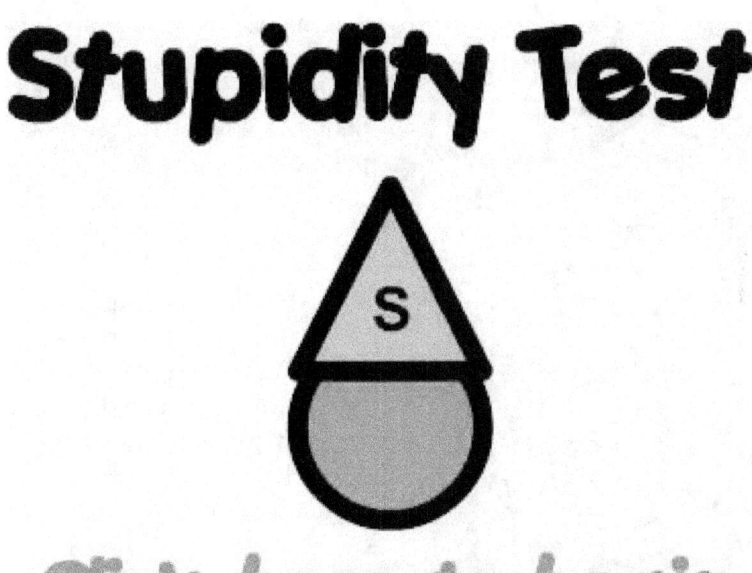

Stupidity Test

Click here to begin

What Specifically can Repugnicants do to prevent a possible invasion of terrorists plotting to overthrow America?

• Question From: Ron Sacino, Bricklayer, Clayton MO

The Truth According to The Repugnicant Babble:
According to our research, there is a close causal relationship between heightened obsession with possible terrorist attacks and the lack of other countervailing paranoias in your life. According to our recently published study, if a person is fearful, angry, upset or otherwise in a charged emotional state, it increases the probability by 19.36% that their brainwave patterns, will descend in a downward spiral of stressful thought and pave the way for a terrorist intrusion into your mind. This so-called Manfred-Wilkenson hypothesis (named after the path breaking research team leaders) has profound implications for our ability to fight terrorism both internally and externally. For example if you let yourself get paranoid about other things, this paranoia will offset terrorism paranoia.

Net Net: you will not become as anxious about terrorism... if you fight terrorist paranoia by getting paranoid about something else ...

... like littering.

Why are Democraps So Elitist?

• Question From: Ben Sadka, Dirt Farmer, Aggra, CO

The Truth According to The Repugnicant Babble: Many self-deluded Democraps feel that their candidates are more " honest and intellectual" than Repugnicants, simply because Repugnicance has had a few slip ups during our debates, public statements and other incidental matters. Obviously, Democraps are elite snobs.

... and this is their way of trying to rationalize their sorry plight by portraying themselves as "intellectually superior." Unfortunately this perception has taken hold in some portions of the "liberal" media, and so we caution all Repugnicants against appearing "intellectual" in public. Not only is being intellectual a futile gesture for Repugnicants, but it is also a risky maneuver, because it will expose you as members of the resistance. Intellectuality will soon become a vestige of previous civilizations on earth, but until that glorious day, we must be careful how we appear. As we perfect our abilities of insincere manipulation in both our public and private personas, we are doing our part to insure that the overpowering forces of pretense and manipulation have their way. Now some of you of may find yourself regressing into intellectuality occasionally. If this happens with any degree of frequency, we recommend using our own branded product, the Repugnicance Insincerity Keyboard. It comes equipped with a virtual undo key that works for events in real life, so if you slip up and by being intellectual, you can simply press the undo button. We consider it to be the killer app for the age of the Repugnicance Movement. ... buy one on Amazon.com ... search for "Repugnicance."

What is the Official Repugnicance Stance on Preventive Dentistry?

• Question From: Ruth Wysoki, Grocery Clerk, Thompson Falls, Montana

The Truth According to The Repugnicant Babble:
This has been on many of our minds lately, even though you don't hear a lot about in the mainstream media, obsessed as they are with other obsessions. This is an often-overlooked threat – the increasingly pervasive effects of

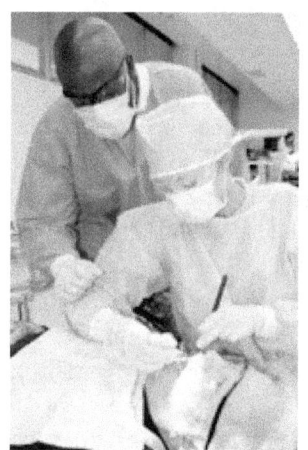

terrorists in our midst using deceptive dental care. While the connection between terrorism and dentistry may seem farfetched to some, it recently came under the scrutiny of the CIA and Department of Homeland security when they received an anonymous tip that some terrorists were carrying nuclear bombs in their cavity fillings. We need to caution you that dentists may soon be disallowed from practicing their craft as the potential terrorist implications of their activities becomes more widely publicized and

understood.
Quality dental care may be difficult to come by, as terrorist alerts become more frequent and specific in tone. We strongly recommend having your cavities filled now, while dentistry is still a viable profession. Repugnicance has been on top of this issue for time now and when we

win the Presidency, we plan to introduce a plan to deal with this issue forthrightly and immediately, without increasing the budge deficit.

What can Repugnicants do about Reality?

• Question From: Xavier Jones, Landscaper, Lancaster, PA

The Truth According to The Repugnicant Babble:
The question of reality is not new to medical and psychological science. What is new, however, it the incidence of reality attacks since the election of Barack Obooma. A recent study presented credible evidence that over 80% of Democraps and 43% of

Repugnicants had had at least one reality attack in the last two days. The average now for a "normal" American is four reality attacks a week, with a slight decline on Saturdays and a frightening spike in the incidence rate during the time when liberals are not in church worshiping on Sundays. If you feel a reality attack coming on, sit quietly in the fetal position, and let your mind wander vacuously as if your were reading, "My Pet Goat" to a classroom of third graders. Soon you will find your brainwave patterns tuning into the brainwave patterns of other third graders, and you will begin to achieve a heightened awareness of what is really not happening in the world. After a comfortable gestation period, begin chanting quietly, "Reality is more than a collective hunch." Do this over and over for at least eight minutes until a mysterious calm comes over you. During this ritualistic ceremony, you may also wish to visualize Repugnicance-esque nirvana. Add tofu, marinate lightly and pan fry the image. For best results, serve with a garnish.

WHAT IS THE BEST WAY TO ROOT OUT SUBVERSIVES FROM WITHIN OUR SOCIETY?

• Question From: Ruth Poop, Secretary, Madison WI

THE TRUTH ACCORDING TO THE REPUGNICANT BABBLE:
The best way to root out subversives is to support Repugnicant's proposed legislation to expand the Patriot Act "To Include Liberals as Terrorists." If you're like most Repugnicance Patriots, you have trouble sleeping in

fear that desperate liberals and Democrapic subversives are now working towards a dismantling of the American values and our fabric of life. We all pray fervently for the fate of our nation and then leave voice and email messages with other Repugnicants seeking to create a viral effect of paranoia. Eventually these prayers and voice mail messages will be transmitted wirelessly to the Repugnicance Database, which will be included and funded by the Repugnicance Patriot Act. We will then transmit these paranoid messages to God, who will act through his omniscient powers to create a groundwell of political support for a much needed redefinition of civil liberty.

What Can We Do To Make Sure That "New Religions" Don't Take Over the Minds of our Nation's Impressionable Young People?

• Question From: Alexander Turnip, Retired Schoolteacher, Havre, Montana

THE TRUTH ACCORDING TO THE REPUGNICANT BABBLE: You hit the nail on the head with this question. Many of us "saved" Americans are beginning to fear that non-believers masquerading as "spirituals" are undermining the faith our country has invested in more "conventional and tested" religions like ours. These "new religions" include Episcopalians, Unitarians, Catholics, Protestants and other media cults like baseball, football and reality TV.

Frankly we are deeply concerned especially about our young people, many of whom practice these new religions and their rituals on sports teams and frat parties. This is a clear violation of the constitutional separation between church and state. Our goal is to have these new "spiritual sports" banned through a constitutional amendment. If you agree with our position, consider supporting the Repugnicance "new messiah" award, which is presented annually at the Baptist Retreat Center is Paukanauee, Arkansas over Memorial Day weekend.

Does Repugnicance Support Interplanetary Settlements and If So Will We Be Able to Buy Real Estate On Mars When a Repugnicant is Elected President?

• Question From: Gertrude Longfellow, Registered Nurse, Staples, Minnesota

THE TRUTH ACCORDING TO THE REPUGNICANT BABBLE: This is an insightful question. We are especially glad you asked it because many "Democraps in Denial" simply refuse to accept the inherent promise of interplanetary exploration. Fortunately, Repugnicants, lead by the inestimable Snoot Gingrich, obviously "get it." Snoot not only grasps the psychic value and technological spinoffs of this Mars Mission, but he also understands the lucrative business opportunities therein.

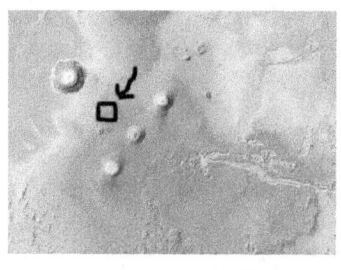

This is why we have joined together with an unnamed Repugnicant campaign donor, who name rhymes with Coke to form a the R-REIT (Repugnicant Real Estate Investment Trust) specifically to market promising real estate opportunities on Mars. A mere $50,000 down and you're in the game, with a picturesque craterside plot of land, spacious enough to build your "castle in the sky." Obviously the coming population shift to the Red Planet will be huge ... with far reaching implications for our economy and lifestyles. This is but one of the many reasons that we need to develop both political and marketing support for Snoot's visionary "mission to Mars" initiative and his accompanying R-REIT. Furthermore, we believe that if Democraps and terrorists continue with their malevolent strategies on earth, Mars may be the only place for Repugnicants and mainstream Americans to live safely. Some of the bugs of interplanetary travel have yet to be worked out, but with enough government funding we believe that within a "reasonable" window of time it will not only be possible to inexpensively travel to Mars, but that a whole new job creation program will be born out of potential real estate construction and retailing opportunities on not only Mars but many other planets, glaxies and universes as well.

Does Recycling Your Toilet Water Actually Help The Environment as Some Fringe Environmentalists Claim?

• Question From: Betty Mooch,   Tuppeware Sales, Grand Rapids, MI

The Truth According to The Repugnicant Babble: We are not sure about the environmental claim here but we do know that recycled toilet water can be an excellent source of Holy Water for "Repugnicance Purification Rites."

Deeper Analysis: Throughout the ages of history, water has been employed by many religions an essential ingredient for living a fulfilled and holy life. We find this legacy especially appealing as the new Repugnicance fundamentalist worldview renders other forms of spiritual purification less satisfying and efficacious. We would like to focus for a brief moment on the role water can play in making the most of your Repugnicance Experience. We fervently believe that as clean water becomes ever more scarce and precious on the planet, that citizens should begin to think of using polluted water to help amplify the salutary benefits of the Repugnicance Experience. Here's a tip. Simply recycle water from your toilet – to your dishwasher – to your shower – and then back to holy use. Even highly toxic water, when applied in the right places on the body can begin to transmute attitudes and in some cases create a complete transformational experience.   Some people who have yet to be "saved" may have difficulty realizing the full potential of these spiritual purification rites using this technique because of dissonant underpinnings of this cosmological moment. ... persevere until you have found your own form of personal bliss, by creating an infinite loop of cosmic, environmental and spiritual stupidity.

WAS BARACK OBAMA'S ELECTION AN ABERRATION?

• Question From: Wally the Wave, 19, Surferdude, San Diego, CA

THE TRUTH ACCORDING TO THE REPUGNICANT BABBLE: AN EMPHATIC YES!!!! Barack Obooma's election to the Presidency of the Untied State was plain and simply an abortive departure from the norm. Never before in the history of human politics has a man with so many quirks been elected to the highest office in our land's country. Take the example of how he sips beer.

This is not normal. George Bush, who admittedly was not necessarily the ideal personage for the job of President, at least knew how to guzzle. Don't forget about those glowing speeches he made that entranced a nation and world with his mesmerization powers. This is the stuff of demagoguery not to mention socialism. But this begs the question of how he elected himself and Joe Biddle as his sidekick with the support of so many normally common sensical people voting in voting booths. It defies the imagination to consider the root causes of this anomaly. A more plausible explanation of this aberrance would simply to dismiss his election as being "Not George Bush!" If this is the case than what does it say about this country and Repugnicance is general. It is not good to say the least. Much of the explanation about Barack Obooma and his delectability has to do with money. He just flat out fundraised superior to his opponent the aging John McPain until Saint Sarah interjected some life into the campaign. That's when Repugnicant campaign coffers started jiggling with increase promise of victory, which unfortunately didn't happen. But wait to 2012. We'll get them this time. It's a new day for Repugnicance.

WHAT CAN ORDINARY CITIZENS DO TO SUPPORT REPUGNICANCE?

• Question From: Jake Morrison, Physical Therapist, Alexandria, VA

THE TRUTH ACCORDING TO THE REPUGNICANT BABBLE: BUY "REPUGNICANCE" BRANDED PRODUCTS One of the sure signs of a true Repugnicance Patriot is an unwavering allegiance to the values that all us hold so dear. Now you can bring these values into your home as products "Made with Repugnicance" Branded like Soap, Shampoo, Laundry Detergent, Laxatives, Toothpaste, Decongestant, Anti-coagulant and Plastic Wrap. Repugnicance Products Ltd also has expanded the Repugnicance Product Line with a complete line of Repugnicance Cookies, Cakes, Pastries … and don't miss our best selling "Repugnicance Toast, with an image of Saint Sarah emblazoned upon it."

www.ebay.com

Is there some way we can bring Repugnicance into our lives more directly?

• Question From: Joe Jingers, Auto Mechanic, Plano, TX

The Truth According to The Repugnicant Babble:

Many Repugnicants were so deflated by the results of the last Presidential election they began looking for ways to escape reality and enter fantasy scenarios for the future. We applaud this as Repugnicant Reinforcement behavior and have created a technological aid to assist in this process. Our Repugnicance fantasy screensaver jump starts the collective Repugnicant imagination by creating a visualization of the

ideal Repugnicant scenario for America. It literally takes you to a wonderful mental vacation spot, all expenses paid for as long as you would like to sit staring at your computer screen. A mobile handset version skips the more advanced features and goes right to the continuous, Fox news feeds and images. Obviously what we will be seeing here is a breakthrough that trumps what "the liberal media" passes off for news. For example one of our screensaver modules includes images of the Repugnicant's victory celebration and inaugural parade in the year 2012, after passage of the constitutional amendment that gives voting privileges to caribou. Another module has news feeds regarding Repugnicance blast off into space to explore the planet of Pluto. Another screensaver module includes improving economic news including the Repugnicance economic stimulus plan resulting in the creation of 2 million new jobs, a balanced budget and an expanded bridge to nowhere. A word of warning though. Apparently some screensavers have been hacked and a truly delusional look at an America has been inserted, in which Wall Street surrenders to Main Street and the Occupy Movement seizes the banks and hires former Wall Street bankers as janitors in public schools. With that one caviar we highly recommend these handy screensaver modules. Repugnicants can reinforce their positively psychotic visions in their own mind. So we urge all Repugnicants to download this screensaver at www.Repugnicance.com and live imaginatively in the illusory world any true Repugnicant would really want to live in.

What, If anything, Should Repugnicants Read?

• Question From: Ruth Cannister, Bookkeeper, Richmond, VA

The Truth According to The Repugnicant Babble: This is the perfect example of a gotcha question, put forth by the mainstream media to detract from Repugnicance. We are modern religion-lite, and most books (even comic books) are much too long. The Repugnicant National Uncommittee does not recommend reading anything other than t-shirts, bumperstickers and tweets. Anything longer than 140 character is extraneous and can cause the Repugnicant mind to buckle. That said we recommend wearing glasses to give the appearance of erudition. Take Saint Sarah for example. She doesn't need to wears glasses, but she does! When asked what he regularly reads, P. Rick Perry anticipated the trap and said sagaciously "all of them" so as not to be typecast as a rote conservative or even worse, a liberal.

STUPID QUESTIONS FOR EVEN STUPIDER REPUGNICANTS

Buy a Repugnicance Brand "Stupidity Siphon" Home Starter Kit

We have received an exclusive tip that the Repugnicant's Church of Transcendent Stupidity has recently reached an agreement with a major defense contractor to begin offering a "Repugnicant Brand" "Stupidity Siphon" Home Starter Kit.

This will be marketed through major retail outlets such as Wal-Mart, Best Buy, Sears and Macys. It will be positioned as a 21st Century version of the home bomb shelter that was all the rage in the 1950's. One of the many intriguing items in the starter kit will be a simple but elegant device that enables ordinary citizens to harvest rainwater for emergency drinking supplies by employing inexpensive plastic tubing to create a "Premium Grade Stupidity Siphon." This ingenious device collects rainwater in buckets (placed at the bottom of drain spouts), siphoning water upwards towards 50-gallon drums (available also in 100 gallon and 500 gallon sizes) to be placed on your roof. The drums can, if properly contoured be used alternatively for hotubs and bathing. We recommend using the stupidity siphon as a metaphor for the Repugnicant Experience, creating a closed loop of infinite societal stupidity. In this way, Repugnicants can recycle their premium grade stupidity so that it can be used repeatedly by other Repugnicants.

Host a Repugnicance Patriot and Paradigm Bonding Party

Proper bonding techniques are essential for worshipers of the Repugnicance Experience. But two perplexing questions present themselves: who to bond with and how? For those of discriminating taste, we recommend hosting a Repugnicant Patriot and Paradigm Bonding Party.

The social benefits of these gatherings can be infinitely heightened with extended debate over the best approaches towards anti-terrorism, the most effective economic stimulus programs and what guns to use when hunting wolves from helicopters. Once the pizza arrives, be sure to stop talking and stare vacuously at the image of Repugnicance, which is now creeping into your mind.

Use The Repugnicance Bonding Signal

To realize the full potential of your Repugnicant Experience, sometimes playful antics can help. Towards this end we have developed a few tricks that you might want to try out on your friends, neighbors and colleagues at board meetings and church services. Our favorite trick is one that comes directly from the Repugnicant's Patriot Playbook. While we are slightly uncomfortable with the self-promotional aspects of this, it is nevertheless fun. So, try the official Repugnicant greeting for "Premium Repugnicant Grade Obedience" bonding.

The greeting is subtle, but unmistakable. Cup your hands up around your face like an excited canine and bark, "Wuff, Wuff" several times. Alternatively, you may choose to use the Repugnicant Approval Response Rating Formula (AARF) and bark, "AARF, AARF" instead. Whenever you see someone in a supermarket checkout line who you think may be Repugnicant, smile and offer the Repugnicance Secret Greeting with a muted barking sound. If they respond with a Repugnicance obedience signal, you have created a lasting bond.

To mentally prepare for the Repugnicance Revolution, we strongly recommend inviting friends and business associates over on a rainy afternoon for a bored game of "Repugnicance Reverse Monopoly."

In this digitally revised version of the venerable board game, participants start with a full portfolio of Bank stocks, US Government securities and real estate assets. But as the economy tanks, and banks get government bailouts, their stocks soar. When the "inflate" card is chosen, federal deficits become so large that the government must default. The stock market then crashes, the federal government declares bankruptcy and all stocks, bonds and real estate assets become worthless. The one who reaches destitution first wins. It's a fun filled way of coming to grips with the potential tragedy inherent in Obooma economic stimulus package.

Exclusive! Buy a Repugnicant brand Self-Composting Toilet

We've developed branded digital self-composting toilet designed to recycle Repugnicant bullshit so that it can be used in future campaigns.

Environmental extremists have long been crying wolf about what they call the "overwhelming stress" human activities have placed

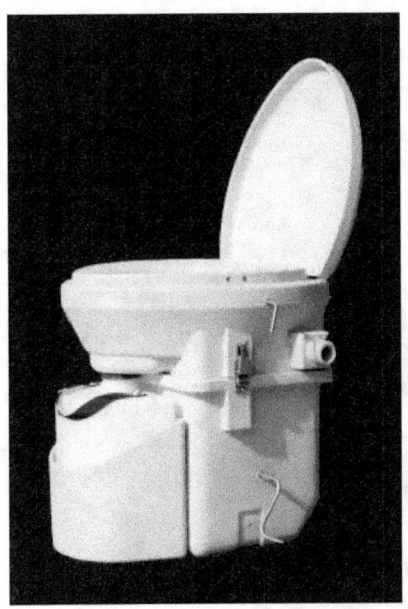

upon our ecological system, but Barack Obama took this one step further with a digitization of the crap that Repugnicant candidates created for the political process with really shitty ideas. He believed that Repugnicant funded public relations efforts could actually be recycled as Democrapic rhetoric. Repugnicants poo-pooed the idea, but the ultimate Democrap, Al Bore was determined and hired a development team which outsourced production of these digital self composting toilets to a factory in China.

Needless to say the idea tanked as did Al Bore's campaign and Al Bore ordered the Repugnicants to get rid all the toilets before word got out about them. P. Rick Perry had em all delivered to his place and stored them in the barn on his ranch. That's where they sit now. Today their all filled with intellectual Democrapic BS, including rhetoric about the need for reduced defense spending, getting rid of tax cuts for the rich and reduced anti-terrorism campaigns. Their designed to be flushed vigorously and often.

PARTICIPATE IN THE "NEWT" GLOBAL ECONOMY BY PURCHASING PREFERRED STOCK IN U. S. INC.

Many insightful economists have been saying that The Obooma economic brain mistrust will cause a complete unraveling of he global economy. Of course, we strongly endorse this position and urge Repugnicant Patriots to prepare for complete transfer of all assets from Main Street to Wall Street with another one of Newt Gangrene great ideas: the formation of U.S. Inc. with a major IPO shortly after the election. This structure is patterned after Saint Sarah's conversion into a cash out model. Consider the upside in this wonderful new phase of history. Stock in many major corporate entities like Bank of America, Goldman Sachs, GE and Citicorp will be exchangeable with shares in this great country of ours.

This will then create an opportunity to think anew in constructing more healthy and enduring financial instruments and economic relationships. Soon the entire U. S. economy will simply be a subsidiary of U.S Inc. and all Repugnicant Patriots can become stockholders with all the privileges of ownership. Get in on the ground floor of this exciting venture by purchasing "preferred" shares in our coming IPO and watch the value of your assets pop on the opening bell. Then sail away on the USS Repugnicance, to the dream destination of your choosing.

Embrace Repugnicant Fantasy As The Real Reality

Many liberals whine about the increasing levels of aberrant power held by Perry Patriotism in the cosmic mind. They blather about the awesome power of the Repugnicance book marketing steamroller in its ability to manipulate public opinion and distort the current state of reality.

But who is really at fault here? The Democraps conveniently forget that they seized power by creating their own reality adjustment machines and fundraising steamroller using the Internet. Lost in all this feverish financial activity is the significance of a reality that has now been trumped by the power of public relations. We all can celebrate our triumph in rendering obsolete the dubious proposition that reality is real. Consider the possibilities as we continue to perfect our tools. Soon the media pundits will no longer be able rail against a political process that distorts, diverts and distracts us from fundamental issues, because the fundamental issues will seem trivial and the trivial issues will seem paramount. Ultimately we will all be able to embrace fantasy without any misgivings, and we will have arrived at a world in which nobody pays any attention at all to what is really happening. Instead we will all have achieved what the even the Democrapic mystics have long held out as the final answer: perpetual unreality. There is one possible glitch however: the future may not arrive. But even if this happens we will all, of course have the option of switching channels, to reality TV.

Support Repugnicant Sponsored Legislation Calling For Christian Tracking Of Potential Terrorists

Modern scientific research has clearly proven that very few Americans have fully accessed their "ultimate" Christian abilities.

If the fundamentalist Christian majority was to collectively access its true potential, we believe, that America would be better prepared to anticipate and foil terrorists before they did any harm to humanity. To help implement this program, we plan to work through our operatives to introduce a rider to the Defense Department Appropriations Bill That earmarks $7.8 billion in the upcoming Federal Budget for insurance discounts to people who have enrolled in a "government sponsored" Christian development course and scored high enough on a standardized Jesus test to qualify as a "Christian field marshall." These protectors of our safety, will be trained and supervised by Repugnicant evangelical Christians, so that they are adequately prepared patrol our streets on a watchful lookout for telltale signals of terrorist activity. Although Christian communication is not always reliable, our research shows, beyond a shadow of a doubt, that Christian predictions can not only help predict terrorist activity, but help forecasting weather, mood swings and traffic congestion patterns.

JOIN IN THE REPUGNICANCE INITIATION RITES TO THE POST MODERN ERA OF EVOLUTION

To hear most Americans speak these days, they are so depressed by the election of Barack Obooma that they see it as a return to a primitive era of civilization when cavemen and apes roamed the earth and tried to rule on the basis of brute force alone. They augment these fears by still looking at their old George Bush chimp pictures. We feel these fears are extreme. Obviously we have a different view of the future.

We think of the Repugnicance as an initiation rite into the postmodern era. The postmodern era, for those who may have flunked anthropology, is a dawning of humanity in which all humans are enlightened creatures, who live happily ever after in their mansions and castles. The initiation rites of the Repugnicance Experience can be likened to the pre-snoring phase at frat party hazing rituals. Unlike other initiation rites throughout this passage in time, theses rites are "totally unique" in that they help to reconcile traditional creationist theories with the existence of more highly evolved humans like Repugnicant Patriots.

THE COMING REPUGNICANCE REVOLUTION

Only the Gospel of Repugnicance can reverse the decline in national morality. Through rigorous pursuit of conservative values, you and yours will wake up and summon your Repugnicant gumption. In other words ... vote with your wallets ... send a check to your the Repugnicant National Uncommittee so that the voting booth in November 2012 will become the ticket to freedom, liberty, growth, prosperity, a strong military and limited government for all.

Many Repugnicants are still doubtful about the current version of Repugnicance in full view of the national citizenry. They are hopeful that somebody ... anybody ... but these candidates will materialize ... to bring if a full-scale transformation of the market based economy before the coming collapse of humanity. But before you get too excited by the vision of the perfect Repugniant candidate materializing before your eyes, consider this cosmic questions: Will the nature of the coming change cause a change in the nature of change itself?

In the old version Repugnicant Babble, some doubters said, that the Repugnicant official position was always changing. This is blasphemy! ....
and it's false too. Since God's has now passed on the gospel to us, there are three thing that matter f o r Repugnicants: lower taxes, s m a l l e r government .... and what was the third thing

... let's see ... lower taxes ... lower taxes and .... what was the third thing? .... I'll think of it ... Oops.

FOLLOW THE RAPTURE

DIRECTIONS TO THE REPUGNICANT

NATIONAL SHRINE

Looking for Repugnicant Rapture? Just follow these directions ... 23 miles due southeast of God's Country ... drive 14.7 miles until you see a pile of empty beer cans. Left at the 5th telephone pole. Sharp right after the big rock. Right onto the dirt road about 5-10 miles until you see a jackrabbit (or is it a possum?) You can't miss it!

When you finally get to the Repugnicance National Shrine, you will see a Perry or a Mitt or a Newt or something resembling a political, standing there in solitary statuary splendor. We invite you to celebrate your arrival, by taking a pee on the candidate of your choice.

There is more to this Repugnicant Shrine than can be seen with the naked eye. Deep beneath the surface of superficial impressiondom, you will behold the stupidity of it all. The Repugnicance National Shrine is our humble way of reminding you that, **"It is not enough to think stupid thoughts."** We at the Repugnicant National Uncommittee believe it is imperative for us to "walk our stupid babble." We recommend taking your stupid Repugnicant babble out open into the wide-open spaces where it can run free. In restricted areas use a leash. If your stupid Repugnicance Babble makes a mess, be sure to clean up after it.

One more thing. Plan to attend the annual Repugnicance Shrine annual hoopla held at Repugnicance shrine the weekend closest to February 29th each year. It's sort of like Burning Man, but without all the psychedelia. Just all of us Repugnicant Patriots, believing that America one one day can and will again become all it can become.

In the final analysis, The Repugnicance Shrine stands out as a cosmic symbol of hope in a vast wasteland of political vacuousness. This kind of powerful symbolism comes only once in the life of a planet, and is the source of all true rapture. Moreover, the Repubnicant Rapture is the cosmically correct frame of mind. To align yourself cosmically with the universe we recommend giving in totally to the cosmic forces of Repugnicant Manifest Destiny so beautifully captured by the artists who rendered the Shrine thingamajig.

It reminds me of that saying, "When it comes to Repugnicance, the only smart thing to do is to be stupid. .... and the only stupid thing to do is to be smart." So make the pilgrimage and tell your friends on Facebook. Tweets welcome. We strongly suggest that you begin spiritual preparations for the Repugnicat Revolution now before the paint dries. Good night and good luck! And remember the Repugnicance rallying cry ...

"REALITY IS OVERRATED!"

TALKING POINTS: Repugnicance is going viral. Use these links as touchstones to the rapture.

REPUGNICANCE ON FACEBOOK

HTTP://WWW.FACEBOOK.COM/PAGES/ REPUGNICANCE/332293770120032

REPUGNICANCE ON TWITTER @REPUGNICANCE

REPUGNICANCE ON GOOGLE+

HTTPS://PLUS.GOOGLE.COM/B/ 108445014202924877393/

About the Author - George Won't

George Won't is the anthesis of George Will. George Will writes for the bastion of the political establishment, *The Washington Post.* George Won't scribbles at the armory of political irreverence, *The Washington Pissed.*

George Will is the consummate Washington insider. George Won't is the ultimate political outsider.

George Will is the master of syntax and grammatical etiquette. George Won't don't give a rats ass about choosing politically correct words. Fact is George Won't don't even care about proper spelling, periods, commas and other etraneous punctuals.

George Will was educated in the Ivy League and circulates with aplomb through Washington society circles. George Won't picked up what he knows at Avery's Barber Shop on Fourth Street. "Hell no!"... You'll never see him wearing a tux, 'n you'll never see George Won't sittin' with the power elite at DC dinner parties. George Will wears bowties ... George Won't don't wear no ties.

At Georgetown parties George Will knows how to hold utensils all prim and proper. He daintily picks up food for thought and skillfully inserts choice morsels of gossip into his widely read columns.

George Won't stuffs food in his mouth with his fingers just like the rest of the locals at the Squat and Gobble in Paint Creek, just outside of town. He listens good to what common folk is saying and somehow works it into wordage that nobody will cherish forever. Dont for get to read George Won't authoritative companion book . Repugnicants: The Wacky World of Republican Politics ... Whatever?

Repugnicants

The Wacky World of Republican Politics

Featuring:

Snoot Gingrich, Snit Romney, Run Paul,
P.Rick Perry, Michele Babblethump,
Herman Pizza and Donald Dump

Edited and Curated by

George Won't

Columnist for the *Washington Pissed*

***

Follow Repugnicance on Twitter @Repugnicance

To order additional copies of this book visit:
www.repugnicance.com

To read George Won't's blog visit:
www.repugnicance.com

For additional information or
for discounts on bulk orders email:

Info@Repugnicance.com

***

Repugnicance Mercantile

http://www.cafepress.com/Repugnicance

www.ingramcontent.com/pod-product-compliance
Lightning Source LLC
Chambersburg PA
CBHW060204290526
45789CB00003B/1154